Forex Trading Strategies

Simple Proven Trading Strategies – That you can Start Making Money Today

Timothy S. Tudor

Timothy S. Tudor

and utter responsibility of the recipient reader. Under no circumstances will any legal responsibility or blame be held against the publisher for any reparation, damages, or monetary loss due to the information herein, either directly or indirectly.

Respective authors own all copyrights not held by the publisher.

The information herein is offered for informational purposes solely, and is universal as so. The presentation of the information is without contract or any type of guarantee assurance.

The trademarks that are used are without any consent, and the publication of the trademark is without permission or backing by the trademark owner. All trademarks and brands within this book are for clarifying purposes only and are the owned by the owners themselves, not affiliated with this document.

Disclaimer

This book is designer to provide information that the author believes to be accurate on the subject matter it covers, but it is sold with the understanding that neither the author nor the publisher is offering individualized advice tailored to any specific portfolio or ta any individual's particular needs, or rendering investment advice or other professional services such as legal accounting advice. Professional services should be sought if one needs expert assistance in areas that include investment, legal, and accounting advice.

There is substantial risk of loss associated with trading these markers. Losses can and will occur. No system of methodology has ever been developed that can guarantee profits or ensure freedom from losses. No representation or implication is being made that using this information will generate profits or ensure freedom from losses. The trade examples provided were hypothetical trading record can completely account for the impact of financial risk in actual live trading. Additionally, this book is not intended to serve as the basis for any financial decisions, as a recommendation of a specific trading system. Your personal financial circumstances must be considered carefully before investing or spending money.

No warranty is made with respect to the accuracy or completeness of the information contained herein, and both the author and the publisher specifically disclaim any responsibility for any liability, loss or risk, personal or otherwise, which is incurred as a consequence, directly or indirectly, of the use of application of any of the contents of this book and any bonus system that are included or referred.

Table of Contents

Introduction

Forex is a wonderful world to be trading in. It is all about money and what do we love to have? Plenty of money to live a comfortable lifestyle. The beauty of forex is being able to invest in the concept of strong currencies. But, with such wonderful opportunities come downsides.

Forex requires a strategy for entering the market, exiting your position, and increasing your profit/loss ratio to show a profit. A proper strategy is paramount to your success.

Anyone can place a trade, but will that trade bring you the retirement fund you seek? The second home? The vacation each year to Hawaii? Only when you have proven strategies based on the various trading methods, will you be able to truly bring in the profit you desire.

You can be the person that trades for 1 or 2 hours, sitting on a beach, with a Mai Tai in your hand. You can be the person that trades before going to work and enjoying your day job.

The retail trading industry has changed making it easier for you to get started in forex trading and enjoying the success you desire. You no longer have to trade with multiple screens, watch the news for hours on end, and eventually make a trade.

It is possible for you to trade 1 to 2 hours a day, on your laptop, anywhere in the world. As long as you have a stable internet connection, and the proven trading strategies you are going to reach success.

Three proven strategies will be shared with you in this book. These strategies are unlike those you have read about before. The strategies assume you have already read through the various types of trends, understand them, practiced looking for them, and tested out your knowledge with paper money trades.

The strategies are going to help you get started trading today. By the time you get to the end of this book, you will have three strategies to follow that allow you to trade in a few hours, make money, and be satisfied with your overall performance for the entire years' trades.

You have what it takes to be a robot trader, without letting your emotions interfere with your important trades. You are capable of viewing the trends, utilizing technology, and determining where a trend is going to go next. You are an intelligent market trader, who understands that waiting for the right entry point in a frame of time is better than rushing in because you "just want to make a trade."

The content of the first section will be specific trading trends and patterns for you to study, so you can use the 3 proven trading strategies to enter the forex, stock, or mutual fund markets. Know that the information in this book may be geared towards forex, but that it can also be used for any market investing you will do.

Investing is all about diversifying. You do not want your entire capital in one currency pair or a conflicting currency pair, such as AUD/USD and GBP/USD, where you could be making money in USD, but losing it too, where you break even versus gaining a profit. Understanding and following the 3 proven strategies ensures you diversify in currencies, stocks, commodities, bonds, mutual funds, and if you wish even real estate.

Chapter 1: Price Action/ Trends

All trading is about the price action a currency pair, stock, or mutual fund is going to take. If you have spent a little time trading real money in the stock or mutual fund markets, then you probably know some of the major trends we are going to talk about when it comes to price action. Some of these trends will be discussed in even further detail in other chapters. For now, this is an overview of price action and trends.

What is price action in Forex?

The price action in forex is called the pip change. A currency pair may move from 1.1456 up to 1.1457, where the price change is 0.0001 pips. The action in this case was a small uptrend in the currency price.

What is a Trend?

A trend is when there is a pattern in the price action that allows you to predict how the currency is going to move from now on. For example, if a currency pair continues from 1.1456 up to 1.496, there is a clear uptrend in the price change, where you are gaining 40 pips in profit. If the currency price moves from 1.1456 to 1.1457 back to 1.1456, then the price is not truly changing. This is called a sideways pattern.

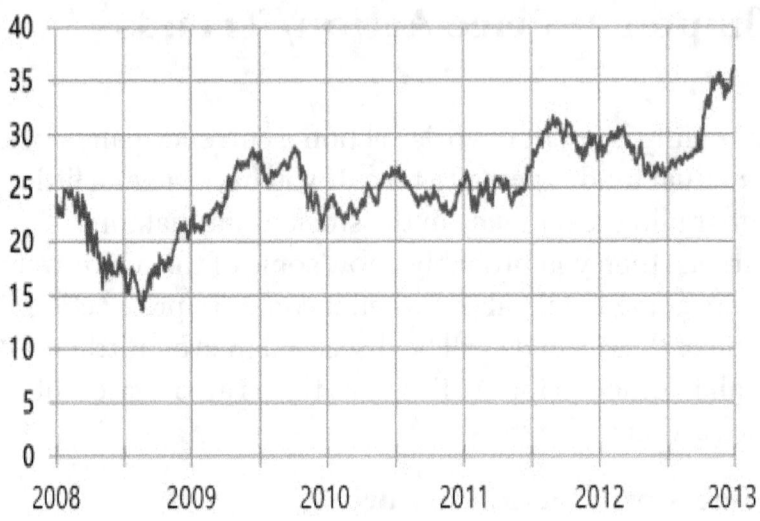

(Image by: Lprd2007)

Take a look at the middle of the chart. Between 2010 and 2011, see how the line is not as distinctive? The price went from 20 to 27, versus from 2009 to 2013, where the price went from 20 up to 35. You can consider a small change of 7 to be minimal, even sideways for that period of time, since the price tended to maintain a 4 to 5-point change, versus a greater change.

This sideways pattern is not something to trade on, unless you have millions of dollars that will earn you a huge profit on a 0.0001 pip change. Mini-lots are not going to earn enough to make a 0.0001 pip change worth investing in.

Best Price Action Trends

- Major Reversal Trends

- Breakouts

- Support and Resistance

- Final Flag (Trend Reversal)

- Head and Shoulders

These price action trends are the easiest to see; especially, for a novice. Utilizing these trends will help you predict the coming patterns and enter the market with confidence.

Major Reversal Trends

Reversals happen in a couple of different forms based on "patterns" seen on the charts. A major trend reversal is where you are going to enter the market based on the new trend. You are hoping the new trend can be ridden to a new high before you exit the position.

The downside to major reversal trends is that a 40% probability of riding a new trend exists. Traders who choose major reversal trends are looking for a low risk position. They want to have a tight stop loss to ensure they do not have a major loss if the market is not going to provide a major reversal.

What to look for:

- You want to look for a trend, whether it is an up or down trend.

- See if there are any pullbacks that will break out of the current channel. A pullback usually looks like two peaks in the opposite direction before the new pattern is established.

- Typically, the current trend resumes for a short period.

- A third pull back will occur where the opposite trend begins in earnest.

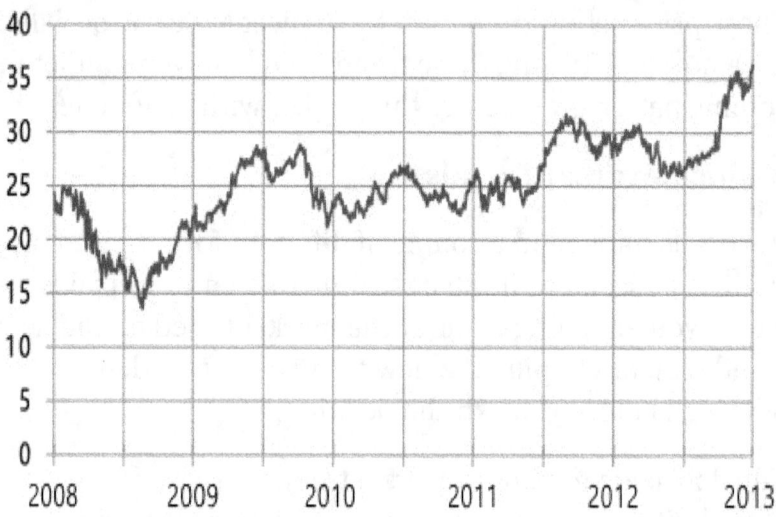

Let's use this chart again. Take a look at 2008 to 2009. At the beginning there is a clear downtrend, but you see towards the end of the trend, there was a pullback with two small peaks, resumption of the downtrend, and then a third peak with resumption of the trend, before a new bottom was hit and since mid-2008 there has been an uptrend.

Ideally, if you traded on this trend, you would have seen the bottom low, but waited until after the price point was higher than 20. Going higher than 20 showed a clear uptrend.

Yes, the profit is less because you didn't buy in at a little lower than 15. However, you knew once the 20 mark had been hit the trend was firmly in place to continue in the uptrend, versus going on a downtrend again.

Major reversals are more easily assessed after sideways travel. Sideways travel is stagnant; however, if you utilize the visible peaks that start to increase in pip difference from the low and high price action, you will see success. Two or three peaks, indicates a trend will breakout from a sideways trend. If you look towards mid-2011, you see on the chart that two peaks occurred, with a dip in trend before a breakout for an uptrend occurred.

Again entering when the high was exceeded, would mean the pattern is clear and it is time to make a profit.

Breakouts

It will be easier to understand breakout trends after spending a chapter on support and resistance. Hopefully, you have at least heard of the support and resistance trend in your beginning forex books. You should know that with support and resistance a clear trend is present, but low and high price points are not broken. Each time the uptrend occurs a certain high is met and the same with a downtrend, a certain low is met. Only when the support or resistance lows and highs are broken, will you see a breakout.

A breakout is a clear pattern where the high or low is no longer met, but exceeded.

What to look for:

- A support and resistance trend.

- Short pullbacks near the support or resistance lines.

- A new high that becomes a short downtrend before returning to the uptrend.

Final Flags

A final flag is a type of reversal pattern, which begins after a continuation in pattern. In this situation, traders expect the current, continuing trend to end. There are indicators on the chart that state a long continuing pattern is going to reverse for the opposite direction, so you can invest in the reversal.

What to look for:

- A continuing trend, one that has lasted for a certain time frame based on the time frame you intend on trading.

- A pullback that is typically a sideways trend for one bar or a short time frame.

- The price is about to reach the support or resistance.

- Other indicators are present, such as a high volume of sell orders when the resistance line has been met.

For example, based on previous patterns, traders may believe the price will not break the resistance, so they begin to sell and sell, thus the trend turns towards the support line again. With final flags, you can trade to the support or resistance line, or set protection orders to see if a breakout will occur.

Head and Shoulders

A head and shoulders reversal can be seen in the same chart as above.

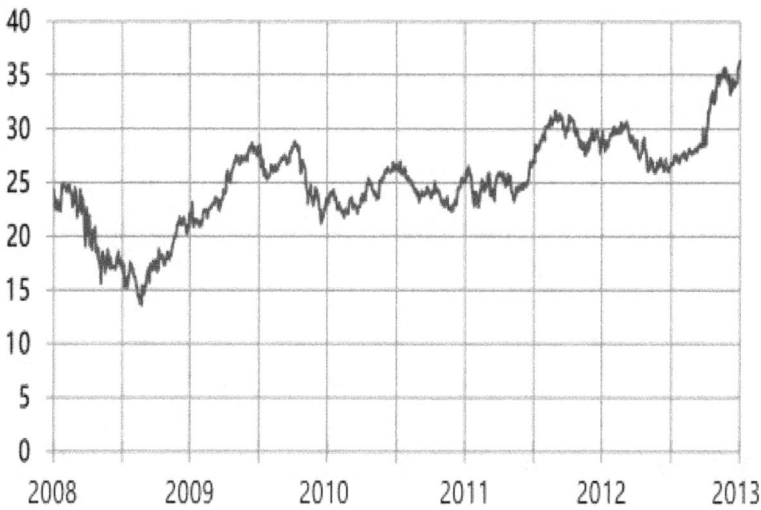

Take a look at 2009 to 2010. See the midpoint of 2009, where there was a small turn between two peaks? Check out the second peak in the middle of the line and 2010. You see how the price went up, dipped slightly, and a higher peak was formed? On the other side, the price dipped, with a short peak, before a nearly same height high was hit as the first peak of the three? Then after that last up, the price went into a downtrend, with a new low before trading sideways?

If you look at the three peaks, between two fingers and ignore the rest of the chart, you will see two shoulders on either side of the high peak (head). Since the two peaks on either side of the higher peak are nearly the same height, they are called shoulders and the high peak is called the head. If you have a good imagination, you can imagine it as a body's head and shoulders.

The head and shoulder trend, does not mean a smooth downtrend or uptrend will occur. Instead, it means a breakout is happening, rather than the continued uptrend or downtrend. A new low or high will be met.

Your strategy should be to exit the market with a trailing stop to ensure you maintain the profit on the trend, without losing your capital.

All of the reversal trends discussed in this section and the support and resistance trend, require you to have "tight stops." A tight stop is where you keep up with the price as it makes a new trend, but ensures you will sell out before a new reversal occurs.

Chapter 2: **Support and Resistance**

Support and resistance trend is the easiest to understand, whether you are using regular charts or candlestick charts. With support and resistance lines, you are capable of setting a trade, with near accuracy of the profit.

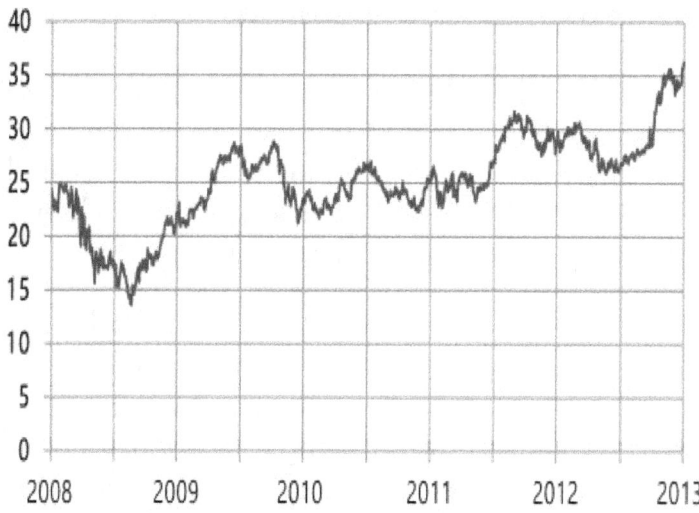

Let's take a look at this chart again, from 2010 to mid-2011. Imagine this time period was a day's worth of price changes. There are several times, where the price went to the resistance line or the day's high. You also have times when the market turned to the support line or the day's low.

If you began with a trade at 2.1000, rode to the resistance line, just under 2.5000, you would make 0.4000 in profit.

You could then wait, for the price to bottom out again at the support line. When this occurs or it gets near that price, you buy back in to open a position. You ride the price action to close to the resistance line again, and close the position.

Why Support and Resistance is Great

With support and resistance, there is usually a clear high and low for a certain trading period. You can determine, based on trend, where you will enter and exit, and the amount of profit you will be able to make.

Let's look at EUR/USD, and say the price is 1.25 as the low for the day. Each time there is a downtrend, the price is around 1.25 such as 1.2510. Each time there is an uptrend the price goes to 1.35 or near it such as 1.3499. You know the difference is 0.1000 pips or close to it.

However, when you set up a trading strategy to make profit on the support and resistance trend, you want a profit/loss ratio of $100. Each 0.0001 pip is worth $10; therefore, you want your trailing stop to maintain only a 0.0010 difference from the market price as the price action occurs.

If you enter the market at 1.2510, then you will set your trailing stop loss at 1.2500. If the price moves to 1.2520, the trailing stop increases to 1.2510. You are now going to break even on the trade, if the price action turns against your position.

You can also set a taking profit order. A taking profit order would trigger a sell order on an uptrend, where you will take a certain amount of profit based on the price action.

In this instance, you might have a taking profit order, where you sell when the price reaches 1.3000. This provides you 0.0500 in profit, versus 0.1000 in profit when the price reaches 1.3500. The idea is to set a profit, without being greedy.

You could ride it all the way to 1.3500, but what if it doesn't make it there? What if you reached 1.3499 and you had a sell order in place at 1.3500? In five seconds after the price reached 1.3499, it dropped to 1.2500 again. You would lose the entire profit.

Luckily, with support and resistance, you can pinpoint the potential profit, set a risk management order, and take a modest profit without losing everything you worked hard for on the trade.

Fibonacci Retracement

The Fibonacci Retracement is a type of technical analysis you can use to trade on the support and resistance, previously discussed. The concept states the financial asset will retrace its steps to the original price. You will have the support and resistance lines drawn on the chart, which indicates price action. A trendline is formed between two extreme points, which is then divided by the vertical distance of the Fibonacci ratios. These ratios are 23.6%, 38.2%, 50%, 61.8% and 100%. The ratios are graphed on the horizontal axis, not the vertical.

Note: Traders feel a break in the Fibonacci levels on the daily close is significant. It is considered an indication that the market price will open in a different trend, such as a breakout of the resistance or support line.

An important number for the Fibonacci Retracement is 76.4%, which is not mentioned. It was thought that if the

61.8 percent level failed and then suddenly headed towards 100%, the 76.4% level would suddenly be reached, and the price would stop before going all the way to 100% retracement.

To make this clearer, the percentages are levels a price will retrace its original steps. If the price started at 1.55 before going to 1.25, it might rise from 1.25, until it hits the 38.2% mark, then fall back to 1.25. If the price started at 1.55, went to 1.25 and returned to the 50% retracement mark on the graph, then turned around, it was generally accepted that the price might continue to 61.8% and to hold rather than set a quick sale assuming the retracement failed. However, if after waiting the price continues towards 100% retracement, then chances are it will stop at 76.4%.

Let's look at a pip/price change example. Say, for two days the GBP/USD increased 150 pips. On the third day, it goes to 75 pips, down from 150 pips profit. Since the price rose, 150, and went back 75 pips, it retraced the price movement by 75 pips or 50% of the original price movement.

The main idea behind the Fibonacci Retracement is to better calculate the support and resistance markers that determine your potential profit based on the market movement.

It is a complicated process for some traders because it requires the use of percentages and trend assessment that may not actually fulfill the prophecy one thinks they see.

Chapter 3: Congressive Trading

Congressive trading is a style of trading, where you have one goal—to make a profit each day. It is not a goal of making a million dollars each day, but rather one where you are looking to stick to your strategy and make a profit based on the entries, exits, and risk management positions you enter.

How to Trade Congressive Style

1. Start with a skill you are comfortable with. Support and resistance are often the most comfortable trend to trade, where you have proven that you can enter the market, make a profit, and close the position before a loss occurs.

2. Use this skill to gain confidence.

3. Set your risk management positions to close before you lose.

4. Keep your trend or pattern indicators simple.

5. Remain disciplined.

As you gain confidence in your trades, you are going to make minor changes to your entry and exit strategies.

These minor changes will help you increase your profit steadily over a long period of time, versus increasing it too quickly and losing your profits each time.

Further Steps

In congressive trading, you are going to start out with a modest profit.

You will trade the same currencies each day, based on the daily information you receive from the news and technical charts.

You will become comfortable with the currency pairs and how they move.

As you place trades, you will monitor the indicators for anything that might work against you.

After, you open a position, you will reduce the tight risk management order, to gain a higher profit.

Gaining more Profit

At the start, you need to calculate how much of your capital you are willing to lose on a trade. For congressive trading, you want a modest, "tight stop" in place, such as 10 pips from the price you entered at. You might say, you are willing to lose $100 on each trade, thus 10 pips, is a good stop loss point.

Once you gain confidence, you will move your stop loss back, perhaps 20 pips from the entry point.

The closer your stop loss is to your buy-in, the easier it is for you to close the position, without doing anything. A simple, quick turn of the trend before a breakout occurs can have the position closed and any potential profits kept from your grasp.

Note: Make certain you are using a trailing stop. A trailing stop will follow the price. When the price increases or decreases based on the trend, you can take advantage of the change, setting a trailing stop, so you get some profit in the event the market turns around and against your current position. You will sell out at the price the currency moved to versus the market price it hit.

You still want to set a comfortable profit margin, without getting too greedy. Make sure the acceptable loss is within your parameters.

As you continue to trade, with risk management orders in place, you will build a profit over the long term, versus millions in one day.

For most novice traders, this is a more acceptable method than taking on higher risks with leverage and minimal capital.

Chapter 4: The 4 Hours and Daily Trend

Forex technology has made things easier in many ways. The 4 hours and daily trend is one of the ways, trading with strategies has become a little easier. There are websites that will display a chart with the 4-hour trend and daily trend.

You should not consider this chart the gospel of currency pair movements., when you are getting ready to trade. Instead, you want to consider the chart as one indicator. It should be used to tell you what a currency pair has done in the past. Before discussing how to use the chart as an indicator, it is best to assess what 4-hours and daily means.

Four Hour Trend

The four-hour trend is either up or down for a currency pair. For example, if the chart says EUR/USD: Up, it means the EUR/USD has been in an uptrend for the last four hours based on how the currency pair opened. If the pair was at 1.1456 at open and it has been up for four hours, it might have increased to 1.1457 and remained there, without moving. Of course, this is not likely. The price might have gone to 1.1467, gone back to 1.1457, then increased to 1.1477. Overall, the trend is up because the price kept rising, even though it went down a little, as the price continued to increase to a higher amount each time.

The Daily Trend

The daily trend can be the same or opposite of the 4-hour trend. Let's say, the EUR/USD opened in Asia at 1.1400, and four hours ago it made it to 1.1477. It has risen 77 pips since the open of the market through the last four hours, so the daily trend is up, and the 4-hour trend is up.

Now for the AUD/USD the price went from 0.4000 to 0.4050 in the last four hours. Yet, at the beginning of the day the opening price was 0.4100. So, the 4-hour trend shows the price increased, but based on the opening price, the trend was actually on a decline for the day. This is why the daily trend can actually be a downslide, even if the last four hours showed an uptrend.

Why is this Important?

The trend is important to the time frame you intend on trading in. If you are going to trade in the next hour, you may see the uptrend for four hours, and assume the pattern will be the same. However, since the main trend for the day has been down, you could buy in on the uptrend expecting a higher price to happen and lose everything you invested.

How to Trade on the Daily and 4-hour Trends

You will want to trade based on the day. You need to examine the complete day, since the market opened in Asia to establish the correct strategy. If a clear downtrend or uptrend is in place, you will need to consider if this main trend for the day is going to continue or if the 4-hour trend has become a turning point.

You need to assess the current trend against the daily trend, to determine if there are any other indicators that suggest the daily trend is about to change. This will take you back to the other trading trends spoken about in earlier chapters.

For example, you might look for the indicators that a major reversal trend is about to occur. If you do not see these indicators, then you may feel confident that the daily trend is going to continue throughout the day and perhaps into the next day.

When the indicators of a reversal trend are present, you can feel more confident that the 4-hour trend is the reversal and the daily trend will become an uptrend, perhaps into the next day.

The only way to be confident in your chosen entry and exit points is to know exactly what has occurred.

It is even possible to say that you want to look at the week's trend before you consider the daily and 4-hour trend.

The reason you might wish to consider the entire week's trading trend is to determine if the current daily trend is really the consistent trend or if it is a short reversal. If the week has been consistently up, the day's downtrend may be a short reversal to a lower value, before a new 52-week high is met.

The more knowledge you have about the pattern of the current trend, the more you are able to ascertain what the indicators are really showing you.

Chapter 5: Risk/Reward Ratio

Do you want to be the guy laying down in the photo?

(Image by: Sira Anamwong)

You probably do not want to be the guy stretching out across the two cliffs and being a bridge for others, correct? It is too much risk. In forex trading, you want to minimize your risk to an acceptable loss amount. The strategies you are going to learn will ask you to keep the risk/reward ratio in mind.

It is generally thought that any trade you make should be a 3:1 reward-to-risk ratio, meaning you have a greater chance at ending up with 3 times the profit of what you have initially invested in the trade.

Let's look at the chart:

4 Trades	Loss	Win
1	$5,000	
2		$10,000
3	$1,000	
4		$8,000
Total	$6,000	$18,000

Over 4 trades, you lost 2 and won 2. The loss is $6,000; however, your profit is $18,000, which is 3 times more than $6,000. Your ratio is 3:1, with a profit.

It is necessary for you to calculate the risk/reward of any trade, before you make an investment.

How much are you willing to lose on a trade?

Are you really willing to lose $1,000 per trade? Can you afford to lose $5,000 on a trade? You really don't want to lose this much, but overall, if you are gaining 3 times more than you lost, you are earning a profit. From the chart, you can see that you made $12,000 in profit based on the 3:1 ratio.

How your Risk/Reward Applies to Pips

Let's say you are putting in a trade for a 3:1 ratio. You have decided that you only want to risk 3 pips in the pip spread. It means the person conducting the trade is going to require 3 pips in profit from you.

If the price is 1.1400 and your trade ends at 1.1403, with 3 pips in the spread for the brokers profit, then you have broken even, not made a profit. To make a profit you would have to see a price change to 1.1409. The market can change in a matter of pips in just a few seconds.

The idea when you are setting up a trade is to maintain a proper risk/reward ratio by setting a stop that maintains your 3:1 or whatever the risk/reward ratio will be. You might decide you are willing to risk 50 pips, so you set a stop. If this is the case, and the pip spread is 3, you would need to earn 153 to meet the 3:1 reward/risk ratio.

The only way to truly gain the profit you desire, is to understand the trends and ensure that as you consider the risk/reward ratio, you understand the acceptable loss factor.

When you set a reward/risk ratio of 3:1, you are willing to accept that you may not get a profit on every trade, but that overall through consistent trades you will see a profit.

By making 50% of your trades profitable, there is a change you can get at least a break even or slight profit.

However, you also have to know the trends you are trading. As part of the 3 proven strategies, it is imperative that you chose a trend you know you can trade on. It is suggested that you look for the support and resistance trend at first. This trend is easier to account for the possible pip increase for the profit you wish to have.

Remember, with support and resistance, the price tends to stop at a certain price, a low and a high price, where you can calculate your potential earnings.

Let's say for 1 hour you see the price go from 1.4500 to 1.5000. This is 0.0500 pips change. In the next hour, the price goes from 1.5000 to 1.4510 and then back to 1.4590 in the third hour.

If you set your entry point at 1.4550 to ensure the trend was going up, and set a stop at 30 profit, you would close your position at 1.4580. True you would not earn 50 pips in profit, but you gained 30. On the downtrend, you decided to sell in at 1.4590, knowing the price would decrease. You set another 30 pip profit, so you closed the position at 1.4560.

In this example, we will say that every 10 pips, is $1,000 in profit; therefore, 30 pips, is $3,000 profit. You set a 3:1 reward/risk and you made $3,000 based on your $1,000 buy-in on the position. In this scenario you kept to the reward/risk ratio of 3:1 because you invested $1,000 for a sure profit of $3,000.

You didn't try to set a stop that was higher, which would have increased the risk of losing, if the price never went higher than 30 pips change. A part of your strategy always has to be setting up risk management orders to avoid the greatest losses.

Once you know how to set the proper orders for risk management, you can eliminate the higher losses.

Chapter 6: Relax, Take a Deep Breath

Trading strategy number one has nothing to do with how to read the charts. It doesn't involve figuring out the fundamental elements affecting the trading platform for the day. Instead, it is about your emotions, and how you should not have any when trading.

(By Isophere)

You might wish to be this guy. He has a boat filled with gold coins and looks pretty happy taking his money on a vacation. The jubilation you feel about making a huge pile of money is certainly going to heighten your emotions.

However, trading on emotions is a no-no. Emotions lead to revenge trading and mistakes.

This trading strategy asks you to correct your emotions before you get into the market. Here is how:

1. Sit down at your computer, at the chosen time you wish to trade.

2. Let the computer warm up, drink a bit of coffee or better yet—tea.

3. Close your eyes.

4. Take a deep breath, in and out.

5. Feel your body start to calm from the excitement, frustration, or any other emotions you are feeling.

6. If necessary, take ten minutes to keep your eyes closed, breathing in and out, and allowing your mind to empty of all the emotions you feel.

7. Once you are relaxed, start your trading day.

8. Analyze the charts for the trend or trends you like to trade on.

9. Determine an entry and exit position.

10. Fill the trade.

It's a simple strategy, correct? It is, but it is also the one thing many traders do not do. Instead, of clearing their mind and focusing on the new day of trading other emotions come into their minds.

Traders reflect on the feelings of the day before or the earlier day's trade. They sit there with numerous thoughts in their mind, such as what is worrying them, frustrating them, or making them uncomfortable.

Science has proven that by taking a deep breath, or a few, while also closing your eyes will relieve you of your negative emotions. The American Institute of Stress states, "deep breathing allows an increased supply of oxygen to reach your brain," which alleviates stress, negative emotions, and fatigue. Closing your eyes helps your entire body to relax, as if you are going to sleep. Utilizing the natural response of your body ensures you can reduce the anxiety, fear, frustration, anger, and other unhappy emotions.

It seems so simple, but why do traders, or anyone else have such a problem following this strategy?

We value our time. We have been taught to think that every minute needs to be filled with doing something, whether it is sleeping or trading. To be idle for even 10 minutes, seems like a waste of time. This mindset is going to work against you more than it will ever help you.

As humans, we also tend to focus more on the negative things. We focus on what we did not get, instead of what we did. We focus on the stress, frustration, and anger, rather than remembering the happiness or calmer feelings. James Gross, a psychologist for Stanford University believes there is a 5-stage model that can be used to help you turn negative emotions.

If you find that taking a deep breath and closing your eyes is not enough or that you need to alter your psychology in situations, then you can take extra steps to ensure you are able to follow this first forex trading strategy.

Improving your Emotional Reactions

Step 1: Select a situation that usually triggers an unwanted response. In this case, you are going to focus on correcting your emotions as they relate to forex. Determine the circumstances that will trigger the emotions. What usually happens for you to feel angry, frustrated, or stress with regards to forex? You might say, obviously, it is losing your profit. You may say it is related to something else in your life that is causing you to have less focus on your trading. The point is not that you don't know why you feel the emotion, but that you will move to the next step to modify the situation.

Step 2: What leads you to feel the emotions you feel? Yes, anger is usually the result when you have lost money, but are you getting frustrated or stressed trying to trade before you even begin the day? Are you hoping for millions in profit each day and instead losing $100,000 per trade? Your positive emotions can actually give rise to your highly negative emotions. In forex trading you need to aim for the reasonable result, versus trying for a perfect trade each time.

Step 3: In this step you are required to shift your "attentional focus." Attentional focus is often about envy. This person's testimonial read *they were able to follow the 10 steps to the strategy in just breathing and make a million on their trade.* This other person stated *they didn't have to use deep breathing because they are never frustrated when trading because they can check their emotions at their office door.*

Yes, maybe the testimonials are the truth, and these individuals are able to do this. However, unless you see the proof there is no sense in worrying about what someone else can do. Instead, focus your attention away from what others have "accomplished," and focus on what you are doing. What goals have you made in forex trading?

Perhaps you have set a goal to simply breathe and relax, and start looking at the market. You start to feel frustrated, so you again repeat the deep breathing exercises and move to another currency pair to see what is happening with that pair.

Eventually, you will be able to focus on what you are accomplishing and feel your emotions retreat.

Step 4: Changing your thoughts is the hardest step. This is a "cognitive reappraisal" step, where you know you cannot change the situation, but you can change your emotional reaction to it. You can use cues that are affecting your emotions to help you recognize the situation and change your feelings before they become full blown disappointment, frustration or anger.

For instance, if you are frustrated with the research you are conducting, you can change the currency pair you are on. You can go back and study the points that are causing you to feel frustrated in order to feel more confident. You can also stop taking too much time on the research, feel confident and simply follow through on an entry you trust.

Step 5: In this last step, you are going to change your response. If you cannot avoid the situation that brings about frustration, adapt your thoughts, and focus on your own accomplishments, then step away.

Take a step back. Leave the room. Listen to calming music, close your eyes, take a deep breath, and wait until you have calmed down from the moments frustration. Try again to research, and find a clear entry position.

Your ultimate goal in forex trading is to trade like a robot. You want to trade without emotions. You want to focus on the entry and exit points you see, with confidence, but without being too happy or focusing on your negative emotions.

Chapter 7: Pick a Trend, Examine Long-term/Short-term Trends

Another part of forex trading strategies that most traders ignore is picking a trend properly. The trader focuses on a small amount of time, rather than the whole picture. The second proven strategy is to look at the long-term trading strategy and then narrow your focus to see how the market is changing over time.

Why do you need to look at the long term?

It might seem silly, if you are trading in 4 hours or less that you should look at the long term. However, this strategy trades on the principle that in a short-term period, you could be missing some of the larger movements that could turn your trend on a dime.

The Steps for Choosing a Trend

1. Choose the longest chart, such as the 52-week chart for a currency pair. Analyze the trend you see. Is there an uptrend, downtrend, sideways trend, or is the trend turning from up to down or vice versa?

2. Move to the next time frame in the chart. Perhaps this one is six months? How has the trend you saw in the 52-week chart changed? What are the trends you are seeing now?

3. Keep moving down in time frames, such as 3 months, 2 months, 1 month, a week, and a day. How have the trends changed? Are you seeing multiple

up and down trends in a day that were not visible in the 52-week chart?

4. Predict the pattern.

The strategy of analyzing the long-term trend before looking at the short-term trend is to learn how to predict the pattern. Traders who can predict the technical pattern are more successful, then traders who assess the charts, without being able to see what will happen next.

Looking at the past can determine what the trend may do next; however, there are numerous other factors that will determine the trend. Focusing on what you see in hindsight versus trying to gauge the next trend or continuing trend will cause you to scamper after the traders who are truly affecting the market.

Tips for Discovering the Pattern

Tip #1: The first tip is obviously to follow the four step strategy outlined above. You have to be able to see the patterns before you can predict them. It takes practice. You also need to know what patterns exist.

The beginning section of this book took you through the various trends. As you studied those trends, you probably determined which ones are more easily understood than others. If you need to, you can continue to study the information about these trends and build your confidence.

Paper money trades are one way to build your confidence, with regards to predicting trends. As soon as you master trend prediction, you are ready to start trading. You may already feel confident and ready to trade today. That is great!

Tip #2: Get appropriate software. There are software programs that allow you to draw lines on charts. For example, you can draw the support and resistance lines, find the uptrends, and determine the current price action by drawing lines.

These lines will help you see the trends more readily.

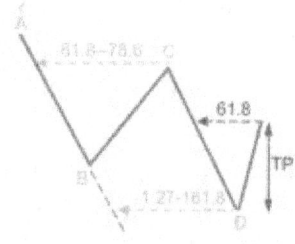

(Image by: یا سی رضا)

Tip #3: Never forget that technical analysis is only half of your trading research. Prediction of trends is only as good as knowing what is happening in the fundamentals.

Many traders make a mistake predicting trends because they forget to look at the giant picture. Yes, predicting trends when you are a large market player can ensure you fulfill your prophecy. However, for those who have mini-lots to trade, it can be detrimental to ignore the bigger players in the market.

One of the most frustrating aspects of trading mini-lots is that governments, central banks, multibillion dollar corporations, and millionaires are trading huge lots. They can choose a trend or try to change the market for a different trend because of fundamental information or because they want to make a profit on a specific currency.

Examining the Long-Term for Prediction

The long-term charts can help you see the big players based on the fundamentals. For example, what if every time Apple is launching a new product, a corporation in London trades in their GBP for USD, but they are changing the trend pattern for an hour?

You could trade with that trend or know that you do not want to trade the GBP/USD. Corporations want to make profit. They want the currency their profit will be in to have more value, just as the corporation spending money wants to ensure their currency pays for more goods. It causes a trend to appear for a short time based on the money or volume of funds involved.

Traders who are able to predict the trend take a great deal of information available to them and make a trade.

The best news for you—is programs are doing a lot of this work for you now. There are several programs out there that will provide you with indicators that predict the market changes.

Step 4 in a Day

What used to take traders days, even multiple hours, is possible to do within an hour or two. Step 4 of this strategy is to predict the pattern. Given the technology we have today; you can now predict the pattern by utilizing software.

Each day, you can begin your trading period by looking at your software.

Investools is at least one program that provides you with indicators. They will give you charts with red or green arrows. If you see three green arrows, there is a strong likelihood that the current pattern will continue or a new pattern will emerge that you can make your entry point on.

Of course, the entry point is still based on your research. You cannot rely solely on the software. You still need to analyze the news, determine what the indicators are, and figure out what the trend is likely to be.

The indicators could be showing a turn in the current trend, such as an uptrend heading down, where you would need to sell short on the currency pair versus buying into it.

With this strategy, you are still relying on your intelligence and research. You are going to utilize the tools available to you, but don't ignore your own thoughts. These robotic thoughts you have adapted from the first trading strategy are going to help you now in seeing the pattern and getting ready to enter the market.

Chapter 8: Wait to Enter and Exit, Don't Rush

Are you itching to trade? Is there anything to trade? Are the currency pairs you are most comfortable trading providing an entry point? Sometimes the market is stagnant. You have seen this already. The currency pair looks like it is trading sideways with minimal pip movements. Perhaps the currency pair went from 1.1456 to 1.1457 and back to 1.1455 in the space of four hours. Unless you have millions invested in that sideways movement, you won't make that much money. Now, if you have a movement of 0.0010 pips, then it would be worth investing because you know there is enough action in the market to make some money on mini-lots.

Strategy three is going to ask you to wait to enter and exit trades, and not to rush. Rushing into a trade because you want to make a profit can cause you a larger loss than you can imagine. It can also ruin the confidence and robotic emotions you are trying to adapt.

Traders tend to make the mistake of investing in the whenever they wish, but not based on the indicators. The second proven strategy is to monitor the charts and look for indicators that will help you predict the market movement.

Now, you are being asked to follow a third strategy that will help you enter the market when there is a point to do so, versus rushing in because you simply want to make a trade.

Let's look at an example. Trader A entered the market on a sideways trend, predicting the currency pair would show an increase in price or make an uptrend. However, the trader entered the market too early. The trader didn't wait for the actual price movement to occur, but entered when the price went from 1.1456 to 1.1450. The sideways trend had the price go up to 1.1456 consistently for the last hour. Trader A was too impatient to wait for a clear entry point. So when the trader entered at 1.1450, they expected the uptrend to go past 1.1456 to 1.1486 based on past trends and market news.

What trader A failed to consider was the 1.1450 price was the beginning of a downturn, versus an uptrend because just as the trader entered their position a news release occurred. The news release stated the projected economic data was worse than predicted, thus everyone waiting and causing the sideways trading trend, began to sell the currency.

If Trader A had waited 10 more minutes, they could have jumped on the downward trend, made a tidy $2,000 profit, and been happier. Instead, Trader A rushed in, tired of waiting, and wanted to make a little money, losing more capital on the trade than should have occurred.

Strategy Protocol

1. Leave your emotions out of the trade.

2. Assess the long and short term trends.

3. Examine current market indicators.

4. Read through the news.

5. Watch the current trend, based on your time frame (investing for 5 minutes, 10 minutes or an hour).

6. Make your move when there are clear indicators your prediction of the trend is correct.

7. Set your protection order to save on the larger losses and maximum profit.

8. Use your protection order for the exit, not your gut.

Yes, strategy one and two are going to be used for your third proven strategy. These strategies go together, so you can ensure maximum profit.

Your actual trade needs to be based on a time frame. You may choose to invest for a few minutes to catch the uptrend on a support and resistance trend. You may choose to trade for the entire day, where you are trading with the day's trend versus the short movements found in a period of 10 minutes. You need to choose a time frame because this is what you are analyzing and predicting patterns on.

It does not mean the next hour will prove to be an entry point. You still have to analyze the indicators. Is this new hour or time frame moving in the way you predicted? Are there clear indicators that you should set up your entry point? If not, can you trade on the reverse indicators, meaning the reverse trend that has appeared versus the pattern you predicted? Is the reverse that is happening stable enough to trade on or do you need to wait for a more stable entry?

Once it is time to enter the market, set up your order to fill based on the price point you are attempting to hit. If you miss the entry that is fine because at least you are not losing your capital. Besides, if your position is missed this time, you can wait for a new position and enter then. It is far better to wait, then to rush in too late to get a profit and end up with a loss.

Your protection order is really the same as choosing an exit point. A protection order such as a stop loss, trailing stop loss, or taking profit order is designed to ensure you get out of the market before it turns against your position and you lose any profit you just made. Trailing stop losses are preferred above all other options. This is because it can follow your position close enough that you keep your profit, without your taking a great loss.

One of the biggest mistakes traders make is holding on to a position too long just to eke out the last pip before the trend changes. This can actually cause you too high of a loss.

Lastly, trading on your gut means you are trying to gain the last pip of profit you can, without truly protecting yourself. Your exit point needs to be set, so you are not rushing out of the trade.

Let's say you are Trader B. This trader entered the market in a great position, has ridden the trend for 100 pips in profit, and feels strongly they can make another 50 pips. Trader B decides to change the protection order. Instead, of the trend continuing it reverses. Now the protection order is not in place and Trade B stepped away. Trader B comes back in 1 minute and the entire profit and capital have been lost.

It is an extreme example, but it is also something that can happen to you. You don't want to suddenly have to rush to close your position because the market is moving against you.

Always have your entry, order protection, and exit in place before you ever get into a trade. It is the strategy that has been proven most effective time and time again, whether you trade in the forex market, stock market, or with mutual funds.

Chapter 9: Tips for Trading

Trading with strategy is simply a way to determine an entry point based on a pattern or trend you see in the price action, as well as having an exit strategy. The tips shared in this chapter will explore a few things you can do to succeed and make money.

Tip #1: You can trade on both up and down trends in the same currency pairs and make a profit each time. Let's say you, entered the market at 1.1456 on the GBP/USD. You rode the uptrend to 1.1496 and sold out. You are taking your profit and leaving it in your investment account. You are now going to take to same capital you started with, invest it again, but this time you sell to open a position. You buy in at 1.1490. You ride the downtrend, which goes to 1.1440 and exit the position.

In the first trade you made 40 pips in profit. On the second trade you made 50 pips in profit. For two trades, in opposite directions, you came away with 90 pips in profit. We will say that each pip is worth $10 because you invested $10,000 in the trade. To calculate your profit, 90 times 10 is $900, meaning you earned $900 on two trades.

Remember the discussion about the 4 hours and daily trend? This is one way to make a profit in a day. In 4 hours, you may have placed both trades, where you made $400 in the first hour and $500 in the next three hours.

You might have traded on the support and resistance all day. Perhaps every hour, the trend changed. You bought a currency pair and sold it at the high. In the next hour, you sold the pair and bought out at the low price. You repeated this until the day ended because the trend never broke out.

Tip #2: Cut your profits and losses short. There is no way to absolutely predict how high or low a price action will go. You can make an estimated assumption based on the trends; however, you cannot say for 100 percent certainty that a currency pair will hit 2.0001 versus stopping at 1.9999.

News makers will say, projections are set for the currency, such as USD, to increase to 0.0050 against the GBP. They may say the USD will hit 2.0000, decreasing against the GBP. Typically, they state, "x currency is projected to exceed the resistance line and hit x price." However, this prediction may not come true. The currency may not exceed the resistance line or it might go higher than the projected breakout.

The point is, you need to set up protection orders, so you gain a profit you expect, not what may happen. You also want to have protection orders in place to ensure your losses end quickly and your profit/loss is always in the positive column.

The idea is to say, the expected price action is 2.0000, so "I" will set up a trade to exit at 1.8900 or exit if the price does not increase from 1.8850, but turns around and hits the stop loss.

If the price goes beyond 1.8900 you would have made more of a profit, but in the same way, 2.0000 may never be reached despite the prediction. It is better to take a reasonable profit than to try to take all the potential profit.

Tip #3: Trade for an overall profit. Losses will happen. They happen to professionals, too, not just a newbie to the market. You want to increase your profit/loss ratio, so you have a positive outcome at the end of the year. Focus on making the next trade profitable, within reason.

Tip #4: Revenge trading is another mistake many traders make. They get into the act of trading with the goal of making what they have lost. For example, you might have set a trade to earn 100 pips on a currency pair. You didn't have a stop loss or trailing stop in place. You lost 20 pips instead of earning 100. Now on the next trade, your mindset is to utilize the trade to make the 20 pips back, plus a new profit. Revenge trading happens when your emotions are heightened. It all comes back to trading without the emotions. You want to be a robot, taking profits, accepting losses, and setting up the next trade to increase your overall profit for the year.

Tip #5: Do not terminate your trade early due to panic. You will want to let runners fly. A breakout that continues and continues is great. It offers you a higher profit than you imagined. However, there is one caveat to this—your trailing stop loss. You never let a runner fly, unless you set a risk management order. A trailing stop loss, ensures if the market stops following the profitable trend that you are able to keep the profit you made. If you let a runner fly, without a stop loss, the market could turn on a dime and you could lose everything you made, plus your capital.

For example, the price of a currency pair ran to 1.9000 from 1.9900. This is 0.0900 pips change. If you sold into the pair knowing the currency would go in a downtrend, you made money, but what if you did not have a trailing stop loss. What if in 30 seconds, the price hit 1.9000 and turned running back to 2.000. Not only did you not get the 900 pips profit, but you also lost another 100 pips. The market can change quickly and without a risk management order, letting runners fly could cost you.

Conclusion

Thank you again for purchasing this book!

I hope this book was able to help you with your needs and to satisfy your reading pleasures.

These proven forex trading strategies should be your guide to making money today. You have already learned about the forex market. Studied various aspects, so now it is time to use these simple to follow strategies to start earning money.

Remember—to leave your emotions out of the equation, allowing you to cut your losses and increase your overall profit. Only when you do not have emotions as part of the trading day can you avoid revenge trading and start making the money you desire.

Trading is always a learning process. The strategy you choose for one trade may need to be adapted for the next based on the market movements. Be flexible, but always have an entry, protection order, and exit plan in place to ensure you avoid the greatest losses.

You are now ready. You have the confidence to trade and the knowledge. Enjoy your successes.

Finally, if you enjoyed this book, please take the time to share your thoughts and post a review on Amazon. It would be greatly appreciated!

Thank you and good luck!